The race, the par........ ,
that never sleeps.
The testimonies, the motivations
that push people to run on the
most famous roads in the world.

No part of this book can therefore be reproduced without the prior consent of the author. Some names have been deliberately changed at the request of those who have given their testimony.

TABLE OF CONTENTS

NEW YORK AND ITS RACE

The New York marathon is one of the most iconic races in the world. It attracts thousands of participants from every corner of the globe. It's much more than a simple 26.2-mile run. It's an exciting experience that captures the soul and heart of those who decide to tackle it.

The road to the marathon can be difficult and challenging, but the motivations that push people to run are multiple.

There are those who run for personal challenge, to overcome their limits and to prove to themselves that they can achieve something great. Some run to raise funds and draw attention to an important cause, to give voice to those who need it. There are runners who commit for the community, to show their support and solidarity towards the city of New York and its people.

There's a special energy and atmosphere that wraps the New York marathon, a sense of unity and sharing those spreads among runners and spectators. As you run down the streets, you meet people of all ages, all nationalities, all cultures, who unite in a single passion: running.

The streets are filled with smiles, encouragement, and gestures of solidarity. There are people playing music, dancing, shouting the runners' names as if they were stars. There are others who run alongside us and encourage us not to give up, who make us feel strong and invincible.

And in the end, when you reach the finish line, the emotion is indescribable: tears of joy, hugs, and smiles that light up your face. You realize you've completed one of the most incredible experiences of your life. At that moment, you feel a sense of gratitude, appreciation for life, and for all the people who have supported you along the way.

The New York marathon is a race that celebrates life and the strength of humanity. It's a run that reminds us that, with perseverance, passion, and determination, we can achieve great things. It's more than a race, it's a life experience. It's not just about running 26.2 miles, but about facing our limits and finding the inner strength to keep pushing beyond pain and fatigue.

It represents a form of personal redemption for a disease that has struck a friend or relative, for the loss of a loved one, for the disappointment of a personal or professional failure. Each runner has a motivation that drives them to cross the start line and face the marathon.

It's the culmination of months of training, of hours and hours spent running, walking, marching. It's the opportunity to prove to ourselves and to the world that we can reach a difficult goal by confronting our fears.

It's not just about running for hours non-stop but doing it with an iron discipline and a winning mentality, ignoring the pain and fatigue that will inevitably come.

The New York marathon is a symbol of courage. It's a journey through life, with its highs and lows, its challenges, and its victories. It's an experience that changes us, that makes us grow. It's a demonstration of love. It's a message of hope for all those who are trying to find the strength to go on.

After crossing the finish line, the marathoner experiences a feeling of triumph and conquest. They feel invincible, capable of facing any challenge.

The love for running, the dedication and passion invested blend into a single experience, in which the pleasure and gratification of having reached a goal that seemed unattainable manifest.

At that moment, the marathoner knows they have won a battle against themselves. It's a moment when the fatigue and sacrifice are repaid with joy and wonder.

From now on, they will know how to overcome any obstacle and reach every goal they set, knowing that anything is possible with the right determination, the right willpower, and the right passion.

A message of hope and positivity, which the marathoner carries with them forever, like a precious treasure, an indelible memory of an epic challenge, a victory that goes far beyond the race.

So, if you're thinking of participating in the New York marathon, remember that you're not just running a race. You're living a unique experience that will change you. You're showing yourself and the whole world that you're strong, that you're determined, that you're courageous. Even if the road will be difficult, never give up. Because you will be ready to achieve what seemed impossible.

BEFORE THE MARATHON THERE'S NEW YORK

The City

New York City is one of the world's most famous and important metropolises. It's been described as the city that never sleeps, offering numerous opportunities for entertainment, culture, and leisure.

Situated on the east coast of the United States, it's divided into five main boroughs: Manhattan, Brooklyn, Queens, the Bronx, and Staten Island. Manhattan is the city's pulsating heart, housing some of the most famous tourist attractions such as Central Park, the Statue of Liberty, and the Empire State Building. Brooklyn is New York's largest and most populous borough, known for its vibrant artistic and cultural scene. Queens is the city's most diverse borough, renowned for its multi-ethnic gastronomy and Citi Field, home to the New York Mets. The Bronx, the northernmost borough, is famous for its zoo and Yankee Stadium, the home of the New York Yankees baseball team. Staten Island stands out for its natural beauty and tranquility compared to the city's other neighborhoods.

New York City offers a wide variety of tourist attractions, including museums, parks, historical monuments, and numerous palaces and skyscrapers. Among the most famous museums are the Metropolitan Museum of Art, the Museum of Modern Art (MoMA), the Solomon R. Guggenheim Museum, and the American Museum of Natural History. Central Park is the city's largest park, a green oasis in the heart of Manhattan. Among the most famous historical monuments are the Statue of Liberty, the World Trade Center Memorial, the Empire

State Building, and the Top of the Rock.

New York City is also famous for its theatre and music scene, with numerous Broadway shows, concerts, and festivals. It's also known for its neighborhoods, each having its own cultural and historical identity. Greenwich Village, for example, is famous for its artistic scene and nightlife. Little Italy is known for its Italian gastronomy, while Chinatown is the largest Chinese neighborhood outside of Asia. Harlem is the heart of the African American community and hosts the famous Apollo Theater.

New York City is also an open-air shopping center where fashion is at home. Here you will find the world's most famous shopping streets. Fifth Avenue with its luxury boutiques and major department stores like Saks Fifth Avenue and

Bergdorf Goodman. SoHo, a trendy neighborhood, with fashionable shops, art galleries, and restaurants.

If you're planning a trip to New York City to participate in the New York Marathon, it's important to have a well-planned and organized itinerary. Once the marathon is completed, you have a great opportunity to explore the city and see all the tourist attractions it has to offer. It's advisable to plan what to see and where to go, so as not to waste precious time.

One of the most famous tourist attractions is the Statue of Liberty. You can take a ferry from Manhattan Island or New Jersey to visit it and enjoy a panoramic view of the city. Alternatively, you can go to the Empire State Building or the Top of The Rock for a panoramic view of New York's skyline.

Central Park is another very popular attraction. You can visit the park and enjoy a walk, a run, or a bike ride along the tree-lined trails. Times Square area is iconic. Here you can find shops, restaurants, bars, and nightclubs. You can attend theatre shows, musicals, and various events.

Finally, you can't leave New York without visiting the Brooklyn Bridge. You can cross the bridge on foot or by bike to enjoy a panoramic view of the city and the Hudson River. New York is a city that offers many opportunities to have fun and discover new things. With careful planning and an open mind, you can spend an unforgettable stay during the marathon period.THE HISTORY OF THE NEW YORK MARATHON

The New York race originates from the queen of Olympic challenges: the marathon run in honor of

Pheidippides, the messenger who in 490 BC ran 42 kilometers from Marathon to Athens to announce the Greeks' victory against the Persians.

The New York marathon, like all other official marathons, is 42.195 kilometers long, officially set by the International Olympic Committee (IOC) in 1908.

This decision dates to the London Olympics of that year, where the marathon was first organized over an official distance of 42.195 kilometers. The length was determined by the need to have the race end at the precise point of Windsor Castle, where English King Edward VII and Queen Alexandra could watch the event from their royal box.

On that occasion, the race length was extended by about 200 meters, equivalent to the distance between the box and the castle gate. From then on, 42.195 kilometers has been officially recognized as the official length.

The New York race is one of the most iconic in the world and has a long and interesting history. It originated informally in 1969 when a group of runners, including the founder, Fred Lebow, organized an amateur race in Central Park. The race, called "Crazy 8s," consisted of eight laps around the park, for a total distance of 11.2 kilometers. It was a success and gave Lebow the idea to organize a real marathon to run in the city.

The first edition was held on September 13, 1970, with the participation of 127 runners. It was won by Welshman Gary Muhrcke, who completed the course in 2 hours, 31 minutes, and 38 seconds. The race took place over four laps of Central Park, limiting participation to male runners only.

In the following years, the event grew in popularity and attracted more and more participants from all over the world. In 1976, the start was moved to Staten Island, with the course crossing all five boroughs of New York. The marathon continued to evolve in the '80s and '90s, becoming an increasingly important race internationally.

Lebow was known for his creativity and his ability to publicize the marathon. In 1976, for example, he decided to have the race start from the Verrazzano Bridge, which connects Brooklyn to Staten Island, starting a tradition that continues today. In 1992, Lebow was diagnosed with brain cancer. He died two years later.

His impact on the New York marathon is still evident today. The race has become one of the biggest sporting events in the world, attracting millions of participants and spectators. Lebow was a pioneer of running, and his vision and passion created an event followed worldwide.

The first winner of the New York marathon was Welsh runner Gary Muhrcke, and in 1994, the new world record was set by Mexican athlete German Silva. In 2001, the race was canceled due to the September 11 terrorist attacks.

Since its first edition in 1970, the New York marathon has seen the participation of thousands of runners each year. In recent years, the number of participants has been limited to about 60,000 runners for security reasons and to ensure the best possible running experience for participants.

In general, it is estimated that about 1 million people have run the New York marathon from 1970 to the present. The race has become one of the most popular and prestigious marathons in the world, attracting professional athletes, amateurs, and running enthusiasts from all over the world. A significant event for the city of New York, with a significant economic impact and great media visibility. The race attracts visitors from all over the world and brings a flow of tourism and economic activity to the city.

The New York marathon is one of the most international running races in the world. Every year, thousands of runners from over a hundred different countries sign up for the race, creating a cosmopolitan and multicultural atmosphere. There are runners coming from Japan, Germany, the United Kingdom, Italy, France, and Australia. However, there are also runners from farther and less represented countries, such as South Korea, Brazil, Argentina, Vietnam, India, the Philippines, and many others.

The cultural and geographical diversity of the participants makes the New York race a unique and special event, celebrating the strength, determination, and passion for running worldwide.

The New York marathon is organized by the New York Road Runners (NYRR), a non-profit organization that promotes road running and other sporting activities in New York City. The entity was founded in 1958, dealing with all aspects of the race organization, from logistical planning to participant safety, from managing registration to promoting the event. The NYRR collaborates with the Municipality and the New York Police and other government agencies to ensure the race is safe and well organized.

The NYRR is also involved in social and charity initiatives, using road running to promote a healthy lifestyle and solidarity. The New York marathon is also an opportunity to raise funds for various charitable organizations.

The Winners

The New York marathon has seen the participation of many world-famous athletes, some of whom have left an indelible mark on the race's history.

One of these is Bill Rodgers, who won in New York four times between 1976 and 1980. Rodgers is one of the most famous runners of the '70s and was the first American to win the Boston marathon in 1975.

One of the most memorable participants was Terry Fox, a Canadian who ran the marathon in 1979 while trying to raise funds for cancer research. Fox had lost a leg due to the disease and ran with a prosthesis. He became an icon of the marathon and the fight against cancer.

Kenyan Geoffrey Mutai won the race in 2011 and 2013, while Tanzanian Juma Ikangaa prevailed four times in 1989, 1990, 1991, and 1992.

In the women's category, the record for wins belongs to Grete Waitz, who won the race nine times between 1978 and 1988. Waitz was the first woman to run the marathon in less than two and a half hours and is considered a legend of long-distance running.

The Records

The records of the New York marathon for the male and female category are as follows: Male Record: 2 hours, 5 minutes, and 6 seconds, set by Geoffrey Mutai (Kenya) in 2011. Victory record: 4 victories, held by Bill Rodgers (USA) and Juma Ikangaa (Tanzania). Female Record: 2 hours, 22 minutes, and 31 seconds, set by Margaret Okayo (Kenya) in 2003. Victory record: 9 victories, held by Grete Waitz (Norway).
There is also a special record called the "Abbott World Marathon Majors Series Record," which considers the

combined times of the Tokyo, Boston, London, Berlin, Chicago, and New York marathons. Currently, the male record is held by Kenyan Eliud Kipchoge, with a combined time of 2 hours, 1 minute, and 39 seconds, while the female record is held by Kenyan Brigid Kosgei, with a combined time of 2 hours, 14 minutes, and 4 seconds.

The Prizes

The prizes for the winners are among the highest. For the 2022 race they were as follows:
First place: $130,000
Second place: $65,000
Third place: $40,000
Fourth place: $25,000
Fifth place: $15,000
In addition, there are also cash prizes for the top American finishers, wheelchair athletes, handbike participants, and winners of the age categories.

HOW TO REGISTER FOR THE MARATHON

There are several ways to register for the New York marathon.

Lottery Registration
Every year, the NYRR opens a lottery registration period where participants can try to get a spot in the race. The lottery is open for a few weeks, and participants are randomly selected to obtain a race spot.

Qualifying Time
Those who have completed a marathon within a good time can use this result to get registered. Qualifying times vary depending on the participant's age and gender.

Fundraising
Participants can get a spot in the New York marathon by fundraising for a charity organization partnered with NYRR.

Tour Operator

Some travel agencies offer packages that include registration for the New York marathon and accommodation and transportation services.

Invitation

Some people may be invited to run the race in the American city at the request of the NYRR. The reasons are various: popularity, sports merits, humanitarian, and others.

How to Participate in the Lottery

Participating in the NYRR lottery to obtain registration for the New York marathon is a simple process and accessible to everyone. Each year, the NYRR announces the opening and closing dates of the lottery. Usually, registrations begin in the early months of the year, but the exact dates can vary. Participants can register through the NYRR website. It is necessary to provide personal information, such as name, address, and contact details. Once registration is complete, participants must wait for the draw to find out if they have obtained a spot in the New York marathon. The NYRR sends an email to all participants who have submitted the registration application with the results. If selected, the bib fee is paid, which usually varies depending on the participant's country of origin.

How to Register with Qualifying Time

To register for the New York marathon through qualifying time, you must have already completed a marathon in a preset time. The rules can vary each year, but generally, they require that participants complete a marathon in a time lower than that set by the NYRR for their age group. During registration, you must provide the qualifying time and the name of the marathon you completed. It does not always guarantee registration but increases the chances of being selected.

Through a Charity
Alternatively, to the qualifying time, participants can try to get a spot in the New York marathon through fundraising by collaborating with a charity affiliated with NYRR. To do this, you must choose one from a list of official entities that have reserved spots for the marathon. Each organization has a minimum fundraising goal, and before registering, it is important to know the required amount. Generally, registration through fundraising requires a registration deposit and a commitment to reach the goal. Once reached, you must confirm registration through the chosen charity organization that will provide instructions and details about the reserved spot.

Register with a Tour Operator: Another option to register is through a tour operator registered with NYRR. In this case, participation is combined with a travel package that includes accommodation, transportation, and other activities. The NYRR has a list of official tour operators who offer travel packages for the race in New York. Each company offers a range of marathon travel packages, with diverse options for accommodation, transportation, and other activities. It's important to choose the most suitable solution for your needs and book the travel package as soon as possible as availabilities are limited.

The Costs
The cost to participate in the New York marathon varies depending on the registration method. The base price to get only the bib for 2023 is $295 for residents and $358 for

non-residents. If you choose to participate in the marathon through a tour operator or through fundraising for charitable associations, the cost may increase. Some packages may include accommodation, transfers, meals, and other activities. There are also other expenses to consider: the cost of the plane trip, the visa (if necessary), clothing and equipment for the race, and travel insurance (highly recommended). In general, participating in the New York marathon can be a costly experience, but many runners consider the cost as an investment to fulfill a dream and to participate in one of the most iconic races in the world.

CATEGORIES

The New York marathon provides several categories of participants.

General Category

It is open to all runners, regardless of gender, age, or nationality. Participants compete for the fastest time.

Elite Category

It is reserved for high-level runners who have been invited by the race organizers. These runners compete for the race victory and for cash prizes.

Disability Category

It is open to those who have a physical disability and want to participate in the marathon. There are various subcategories, such as wheelchairs, handbikes, and prosthetics.

Age Group Category

It is divided into age bands, where runners compete against others of the same age. This category is further divided into subcategories depending on sex.

Charity Category

It is reserved for runners who register for the marathon to raise funds for charitable associations. Runners must reach a certain fundraising goal to be able to participate in the race.

International Category

It is reserved for runners who are not residents in the United States and who wish to participate in the marathon. In this category, there are further subdivisions according to the country of origin of the runners.

Groups Category

It is open to groups of runners who register together to participate in the marathon.

Lottery Category

It is reserved for those who participate in the NYRR lottery for the chance to obtain registration for the marathon.

Time Limit

The time limit to complete the New York marathon, regardless of the category of belonging, is 8 hours and 30 minutes from when the start is given. It's important to note that there are checkpoints along the race route where runners must pass to continue running.

Services and Refreshments

To ensure that all participants have the chance to complete the marathon within the time limit, the NYRR provides various services along the route, such as refreshment points, bathrooms, and medical assistance. Also, participants who run near the time limit are accompanied by pacemakers who help them maintain the right pace to be able to complete the race within the set time limit.

Along the race route, many refreshment points are set up: on average, there are 26 areas along the 42.195 km of the route. They offer water, electrolyte supplements, and often also fruit and snacks to help runners maintain the necessary energy to face the race. There are also medical assistance points, where runners can receive medical care if needed. Numerous bathrooms are set up along the route to allow runners to make a stop if needed. On average, there are about 1,500 chemical toilets located along the route. They are positioned along the edge of the road and marked by appropriate signs. There are also bathrooms inside the start and finish area, where participants can use the hygienic services before and after the race.

THE SO-CALLED "WAVES"

The New York Marathon begins on the Verrazzano Bridge that connects Staten Island to Brooklyn. The race start is divided into three or four waves, with runners starting at 25-minute intervals depending on the number of participants. The waves or "waves" of the New York Marathon are starting groups used to manage the flow of runners. There are four waves at regular intervals from each other. The first is reserved for the fastest runners and competitors who have registered with qualifying time, while the other three are open to everyone else.

The "waves", identified by a number on the race bib, help reduce traffic and confusion on the road, ensuring the race takes place in a safe and orderly manner. Furthermore, the waves reduce the number of people crowding at the start, allowing runners to start the marathon more smoothly and without bottlenecks.

The New York marathon bibs also include letters and colors that identify the runner's start category in addition to their starting "wave".

The letters (A, B, C, D, E, F, G) indicate the runner's starting gates to form a sort of orderly line along the route leading to the start.

The colors (orange, blue, green) identify the runner's starting location: runners with a blue bib start on the right side of the bridge at the upper level; those with an orange bib on the left side of the bridge, at the upper level; while those with the green indication start the race on the left side of the bridge, but at the lower level.

There are also colored bibs for runners who have run the marathon at least 15 times and runners who have registered through the fundraising program.

WHERE TO PICK UP THE RACE BIB

The Marathon Expo takes place at the Javits Center in Manhattan, a large convention center located on 34th Street, between 11th Avenue and 12th Avenue. Thanks to its strategic location and the size of its spaces, the Javits Center is the ideal place to welcome all marathon participants and offer them all the necessary services, such as bib pickup, race pack distribution, and the opportunity to meet industry experts and world-famous athletes.
Bib pickup for the New York Marathon takes place during the Marathon Expo. Typically, the expo begins on Thursday and ends on Saturday before the marathon. Expo opening hours vary depending on the day but are usually from 10:00 to 20:00.
To pick up the bib, participants must show a valid ID (for example, an ID card or passport) and

registration confirmation sent by email a few weeks before the race.

At the Marathon Expo, there are spaces dedicated to conferences and seminars with industry experts and testimonies from world-famous athletes, to provide participants with information and advice on the race and the physical and mental preparation needed to best tackle it.

The Marathon Expo is a much-anticipated event by running enthusiasts and represents a kind of anticipation of the excitement and adrenaline experienced during the New York Marathon.

THE SIDELINE RACES

The Saturday before the New York marathon, the "Dash to the Finish Line", a 5-kilometer race, takes place. The race starts from the center of Manhattan and ends in Central Park. The race is open to everyone, from beginners to more experienced athletes, and represents an excellent opportunity for those who want to savor the atmosphere of the New York marathon without having to face the full distance.

The Dash to the Finish Line is organized by the New York Road Runners, the same organization that manages the New York marathon. The race offers a unique experience, with the opportunity to run through the streets of Manhattan passing through some of the city's most iconic places. The start is in front of the UN building.

The Dash to the Finish Line is also characterized by a large participation, a strong festive atmosphere, and the presence of thousands of fans along the course who encourage the runners.

It starts in front of the UN building (46th Street with 1st Avenue) and arrives at the Finish Line stands of the New York marathon (West67th street with Central Park West). The distance is 5 km. Anyone can participate in the race, both those registered for the marathon and companions, provided registration is made a few weeks before the start.

HOW TO REACH THE STARTING VILLAGE

To reach the start of the New York marathon from Manhattan, there are several options. One of the most convenient is to use public transport, in particular the subway to Battery Park. The New York Marathon guarantees participants free rides for the entire race day. Alternatively, runners can use the free shuttle services provided by the New York marathon to reach the start. These shuttle services start from different areas of the city, including Central Park and Times Square.

In any case, it's important to plan your itinerary in advance and ensure you have enough time to reach the start to avoid the risk of being late, which could result in being excluded from the race.

To reach Staten Island, where the New York marathon starts, you can take the ferry boat that crosses the

Hudson River. The service is operated by the Staten Island Ferry company and is free. The boat leaves from the Whitehall Street terminal in the Manhattan district and arrives at the St. George terminal in Staten Island. During the weekend, the service is intensified to allow participants to reach the start of the race. Once they arrive in St. George, athletes can then take a shuttle bus that will take them to the marathon village at Fort Wadsworth.

To access it, you must go through some security checks. You must go through metal detectors and luggage is carefully checked. In addition, it is forbidden to carry sharp objects, aerosols, and food. The only allowed liquids are those in transparent and sealed bottles, with a maximum of 1 liter each. All participants and companions must also wear their bib clearly visible.

Fort Wadsworth is a historic fort located on the tip of Staten Island.

Built in 1663, it has a long military history and played a crucial role in defending the city of New York. It underwent several changes and expansions over the centuries. In 1776, during the American War of Independence, the fort was occupied by British troops who used it to keep the city under control. In 1794, it was rebuilt in anticipation of a possible war with France.

Throughout the 19th century, the fort was expanded and improved in response to the threat of a war with England and during the American Civil War, it was used as a training center for Union soldiers.

In 1901, it was transformed into a coastal artillery base with the installation of large caliber cannons to protect the entrance to the Port of New York.

During World War I, it was used as a training center for American troops preparing to leave for Europe.

During World War II, new anti-aircraft cannon batteries were added and in the post-war period, it was used as a training center for military reserves and a control center for New York's air defense.

Given to the National Park Service in the late '70s, it was partially opened to the public. Today, Fort Wadsworth is a popular tourist attraction as well as a military base and is known worldwide as the starting point of the New York Marathon.

TELEVISION BROADCASTS

The New York Marathon is one of the most followed sporting events worldwide, with media coverage involving numerous broadcasters. Every year, the race is aired live on various television networks in the United States and globally. In the U.S., the broadcast is managed by ABC and ESPN. ABC airs the race live from 9:00 to 12:30, with national coverage across all states. ESPN, on the other hand, offers comprehensive coverage of the race, with pre-race programs and interviews with amateur runners and the public. Other media outlets providing event coverage include NBC Sports, NBC 4 New York, and Fox 5. Internationally, the New York Marathon is aired in over 175 countries. The race is estimated to reach a television audience of over 150 million viewers. For those abroad, there are several options. Streaming services from U.S.

television networks, such as ESPN, ABC, and NBC, are increasingly available, and many countries have their own linked networks. For example, in Italy, the race is aired on Rai Sport, and in the United Kingdom, it's aired on BBC Sport. The official marathon website offers live broadcasting and allows you to track each individual athlete through their app and GPS trackers. Simply input the runner's race bib number and their last name, and the runner will appear as a dot on the New York map.

THE RACE

The New York Marathon is one of the most famous and prestigious running races in the world. After months of training and preparation, finally comes race day. After months of preparation, sacrifices, and hard work, you are ready to face the big challenge. It's the greatest feeling you can have because you know that behind the starting line are months of rigorous training. It's best to have a well-defined race plan and follow it carefully. This means establishing a running pace suitable to your abilities and the type of training you've undertaken, avoiding starting too fast and risking depleting all your energy in the early kilometers. A good way to monitor this is by using a heart rate monitor or a GPS to track your speed and heart rate during the run.

Be prepared for the challenges you may encounter along the way, such as the hills and descents that characterize this race, conserving energy for the more demanding moments. It's crucial to keep your hydration and nutrition under control during the race, especially in cases of high temperatures or humidity.

Keeping your motivation high throughout the entire race, especially during the more challenging moments, is fundamental. This can be achieved in various ways: focusing on your goals, reflecting on the best moments of training, seeking support from spectators.

Facing a marathon like the New York Marathon can pose many difficulties, both physically and mentally; the length of the race and its challenging course require considerable endurance and proper physical preparation.

THE COURSE

The marathon course crosses the five boroughs of the city: Staten Island, Brooklyn, Queens, the Bronx, and Manhattan. The race begins on the Verrazzano Bridge in Staten Island. It continues through Brooklyn, passing through the Bay Ridge neighborhood. Runners then cross the Pulaski Bridge into Queens, followed by the Queensboro Bridge to enter Manhattan. The race goes up First Avenue, reaches the Bronx, then back down Fifth Avenue and into Central Park until the finish line.

RACE STRATEGIES

To succeed in the New York Marathon, it's important to have a well-defined race plan. Many runners decide to start slow and gradually increase their pace. This way, they avoid becoming too tired too early and can maintain a consistent pace throughout the race. Other runners, however, prefer to start strong and then slow down towards the end when fatigue begins to set in. This strategy requires great physical and mental stamina but can be very effective for those with good running experience. It's crucial to find your own running rhythm and maintain good posture during the race, paying attention to your breathing and trying to regulate it to avoid becoming too tired too early. There's a rule among marathoners: on race day, don't improvise anything. From clothing to energy gels, from shoes to race strategy, everything should have been tested during the long workouts leading up to the race. The risk is to ingest food that can upset the stomach, wear a shirt that rubs against the skin, run with shoes that cause pain, or worse yet, get the strategy wrong and have to drop out for running out of energy. The marathon should be planned days before, kilometer after kilometer, meter after meter, leaving no room for improvisation.

THE CROWD

One of the most exciting aspects of the New York Marathon is the crowd. Throughout the entire course, there are thousands of people (the last count was around one million spectators) applauding and cheering on the runners, creating a festive and supportive atmosphere. The signs bearing runners' names, the drums, the bands, and the dancers all contribute to creating an unforgettable aura.

THE FINISH LINE

After 42.195 km, finally comes the marathon finish line. It's located within Central Park, where runners can finally relax and savor the moment. They will receive a medal and a thermal poncho.

RACE DAY

The day begins with an early alarm, a light breakfast, and a ferry ride that will transport runners to Staten Island, the starting point of the marathon. The journey is long, but the view of the Statue of Liberty and the Manhattan skyscrapers makes everything more beautiful and stimulating. Upon arrival in Staten Island, one heads to the start village, where there are thousands of runners preparing for the race. Athletes of all ages and levels are present, all united by a passion for running and a desire to complete the marathon. The first thing to do is to find one's spot within the starting village. Here, there are tents where you can relax and stretch, or you can sit on the grass and enjoy the atmosphere.

Before setting off, it's important to check the gear: running shoes, clothing, sunglasses, to have everything in order and avoid problems during the race. As the start time approaches, the atmosphere becomes increasingly electrifying. There are speakers who animate the crowd, cheers and chants, bands playing live music. Everyone is there to support the runners, to give them the necessary strength to face the race. Before the start, there are a few important things to do. Firstly, it's necessary to visit the restroom. There are thousands of portable restrooms arranged along the route, but it's always better to go beforehand to avoid inconveniences. Then, one must take the last replenishment of water and carbohydrates to have the necessary energy to face the many kilometers of running. Finally, it's time to start, an unforgettable experience.

On the Verrazzano Bridge, where the first stretch of the race takes place, one can admire a breathtaking view of New York City. To the left, you can see Manhattan with its skyscrapers and the Statue of Liberty, to the right the Atlantic Ocean and New York Bay. This first part of the race, which lasts about 2 km, is very evocative and represents one of the most exciting moments of the marathon.

Staten Island

Located in the southern part of New York, it's one of the five boroughs of the city. This island, about 21 kilometers long and 8 wides, is approximately 5 kilometers from the coast of New Jersey.

It was inhabited for thousands of years by Native American tribes. In 1524, the Italian explorer Giovanni da Verrazzano sailed along the coast and named the area "Staten Island" in honor of his benefactors, the States brothers. In 1661, the Dutch bought the island from the

Lenape Indians and called it "Staaten Eylandt," which means "States Island." Over the years, the island passed from the hands of the Dutch to the British and then to the American colonists. In the 19th century, it became a popular tourist destination thanks to its beaches and panoramic location. In 1898, the island was annexed to the city of New York along with the other four boroughs (Manhattan, Brooklyn, Queens, and the Bronx) to form the modern city.

Today, Staten Island is known for its natural beauty and its important historical monuments, such as Fort Wadsworth and the Verrazzano Bridge. In addition, the island is home to numerous tourist attractions, including the Staten Island Ferry, the Richmond County Bank Ballpark, and the Staten Island Zoo.

Every year, thousands of runners gather at Fort Wadsworth to start their 42.195-kilometer adventure along the route that crosses the five boroughs of New York.

The Verrazzano Bridge

The race starts on the Verrazzano Bridge, one of the most iconic symbols of New York City. It was inaugurated on November 21, 1964, and was named in honor of the Italian explorer Giovanni da Verrazzano, who was the first European to navigate the area of New York Bay. Its construction was a titanic undertaking. The project was developed by the famous architect Othmar Ammann, who had designed other successful works like the George Washington Bridge. The Verrazzano is the longest suspension bridge in the United States and the ninth in the world, with a total length of 4.26 kilometers. It has become a symbol of New York City and one of its most recognizable monuments. The marathoners running on the bridge are an unforgettable image of the race, even though those starting in the lower lane are practically invisible from aerial images.

Brooklyn

After crossing the bridge, the runners arrive in the Brooklyn neighborhood, where they are welcomed by a warm and joyful crowd. Located at the southwest end of Long Island, Brooklyn is the most populous district of New York City and the second largest in size after Queens.

Its history began in 1634 when the Dutch West India Company founded a colony there. The first inhabitants were mainly farmers, growing tobacco, corn, and wheat. In 1664, the British conquered the colony and renamed it New York, but Brooklyn remained an independent city until 1898 when it was merged with the other four cities to form Greater New York City.

During the 19th century, Brooklyn grew rapidly thanks to industrialization and immigration. Many factories were established in the city, attracting many workers.

By the mid-20th century, it was the fourth-largest city in the United States, with a population of over 2.5 million people. However, the city began to decline in the '60s and '70s, due to deindustrialization and crime.

In recent decades, Brooklyn has returned to being a growing city, with a major real estate and cultural boom. It has become a popular destination for tourists and artists, with numerous museums, art galleries, and theaters.

Three Different Paths Based on Bib
Color

Upon arriving in Bay Ridge, a
neighborhood in Brooklyn, the
three initial paths of the New York
Marathon temporarily split
following the highway junctions.
Blue runners reach the right lane
of Fourth Avenue while those with
an orange bib make a turn to find
themselves on the left lane. Those
with green bibs run along the
Gowanus Expressway for several
kilometers before joining the
streams of the other two paths. The
party begins at the seventh
kilometer on Fourth Avenue, with
thousands of people cheering and
singing. The Bay Ridge
neighborhood is a mix of cultures
where the first generations of Irish,
Greek, Italian, and Norwegian
immigrants have given way to
Arabs, Asians, and Russians.

Sunset Park

Runners arrive at Sunset Park, where they can admire the New York Bay and the Statue of Liberty from the panoramic park that gives the neighborhood its name. The area was originally inhabited by communities of Irish and German immigrants. Throughout the 20th century, the neighborhood has seen an increase in the population of Chinese and Latin American immigrants. During the '80s and '90s, it experienced economic and social decline, but in recent years it has seen an increase in public and private investments. This has led to the redevelopment of the park, the creation of new green spaces, and the opening of new shops and restaurants. Sunset Park is also the site of one of the main industries of the New York harbor, with a large amount of commercial activity related to the import and export of goods. It is also home to various cultural institutions, including the Brooklyn Contemporary Art Center and the Irondale Theater.

The Clock Tower

The marathon continues towards Greenwood Heights, a neighborhood named after the nearby Green-Wood Cemetery. The entire area is known for its Federal-style row houses. Additionally, runners will be able to admire an imposing skyscraper, the "Greenwood Clock Tower," about 70 meters high, standing in the area surrounding the cemetery and featuring a large clock on its top. The tower, built in 1892, was originally used as a water reservoir and supplied the entire local community. A few more kilometers and runners cross Prospect Avenue and Flatbush Avenue, dividing the Gowanus and Park Slope neighborhoods. The former is industrial and popular while the latter is renowned for being one of the most beautiful and affluent areas in New York.

Williamsburg

Around the fifteenth kilometer, runners leave Fourth Avenue near the Williamsburg Savings Bank Tower, a building that hosts exhibits and a set for movies and TV series. The race continues along Lafayette Avenue, in the Fort Green and Clinton Hill neighborhoods, where they can witness numerous musical performances, including that of the Bishop Loughlin Memorial High School Band, which plays the Rocky theme non-stop from morning until the end of the marathon.

Bed-Stuy

Runners then pass through the Bedford-Stuyvesant neighborhood, historically considered one of the city's toughest neighborhoods, characterized by high rates of crime and poverty. However, in recent decades, Bed-Stuy has undergone significant gentrification and an improvement in living conditions. The area is rich in African American culture and was one of the main centers of hip-hop culture during the '80s and '90s. The neighborhood is famous for its brownstone townhouses, with elegant brick facades and beautiful wrought iron decorations. It is also home to several cultural and artistic institutions, including the Brooklyn African Culture Museum and the Billie Holiday Theater.

The Orthodox Hasidic Community

At the end of Bedford Avenue, the route moves south of Williamsburg, in the heart of the Orthodox Hasidic Jewish community, where the values of modesty and faith are very important. Runners experience an almost unreal silence, as the community completely ignores the event. The Hasidic community has a long history and a strong sense of cultural identity: it has its own schools, synagogues, restaurants, and shops, and most community members strictly follow traditional Jewish laws. Women dress modestly, covering their arms and legs with long dresses, while men wear traditional clothing, such as the wide-brimmed hat and the long black jacket. The Hasidic community in Williamsburg has also had disputes with the rest of New York City. For instance, community members have been criticized for their refusal to vaccinate their children against infectious diseases, leading to an increase in measles cases in the neighborhood. Some members have protested the marathon, citing traffic issues and interruptions of religious activities. However, in recent years the community and race organizers have worked together to find a compromise and ensure that the race crosses the area without causing significant disruptions.

Williamsburg is a neighborhood located along the eastern shore of the Hudson River. It was named after Jonathan Williams, the first president of the United States Military Academy. Founded in 1827, it was incorporated into the city of Brooklyn in 1852. Initially, it was a residential area for New York's well-off families, but during the second half of the 19th century, it became a major manufacturing center.

Throughout the 20th century, Williamsburg underwent a severe economic and social crisis. Many of the factories that made the neighborhood prosperous closed down, leaving thousands of people unemployed. In the '70s and '80s, it became known for crime and urban decay. However, it was the subject of a major renewal process. Artists and young professionals began moving into the area, attracted by competitive rents and proximity to Manhattan. The neighborhood has become a major cultural center, with a strong presence of art galleries.

The Hipster Culture

The marathon grazes the pedestrian walkway of the Williamsburg Bridge, connecting Brooklyn with Manhattan's Lower East Side, and arrives at Bedford Avenue, one of the global hubs of hipsters, with shops, restaurants, and constantly active people.

New York's hipster culture spread from the 2000s and has had a significant influence on fashion and music. It is generally practiced by young adults known for their alternative look, often characterized by eyeglasses with thick frames, groomed beards, tattoos, vintage clothing, wide-brimmed hats, and a mix of retro and modern styles. They are also known for their interest in independent culture, indie music, art and handmade crafts, organic and sustainable food, and technology.

However, in recent years the term "hipster" has become a subject of criticism and mockery, as some people have seen this subculture as a phenomenon of excessive gentrification. But followers remain an important part of New York's urban society and continue to influence the city's fashion and lifestyle.

The Queens

To leave Brooklyn and arrive in Queens, runners must cross the

Pulaski Bridge, named after Polish General Kazimierz Pułaski. Here, for the first time in the race, one can admire the Manhattan panorama with the Empire State Building and Chrysler Building in plain sight. At the summit of the bridge, the half-marathon mark is passed: 21 kilometers left behind and just as many still to be run.

Upon arrival in Queens, an immediate sort of metamorphosis is noticed in comparison to the city encountered before. The change is evident and tangible. Queens is one of the five boroughs of New York City and is in the eastern part of the city. It was founded in 1683 by Dutch colonists and saw rapid development in the 19th century, with the construction of bridges and roads that connected it to Manhattan and Brooklyn. During the 20th century, it experienced a great population increase due to the construction of low-cost housing and job creation in factories and airports. During World War II, Queens played an important role as a center for war production, with the aviation industry seeing significant growth. In recent decades, it has become one of the most diverse and multicultural districts of New York City, with a large population of immigrants from around the world. There are numerous ethnic neighborhoods, including Chinatown, Little India, and Little Brazil.

Beyond its rich cultural history, Queens is also known for its architecture, parks, and museums. The Unisphere, located in Flushing Meadows-Corona Park, is one of the city's most recognizable symbols and was built for the 1964 World's Fair. The Museum of Modern Art of New York, the Museum of Natural History, and the Queens Museum of Art are just some of the world-renowned cultural institutions found in Queens. It also hosts two airports: John F. Kennedy International Airport and LaGuardia Airport, making the borough a significant gateway for visitors from around the world.

The New York Marathon route passes through the Long Island City area, where a new residential area is emerging that has erased the famous Five Pointz, an industrial complex covered in graffiti. After running along Crescent Street, the runners tackle the Ed Koch Queensboro Bridge, one of New York's most famous bridges, which connects Queens to Manhattan and spans over the small Roosevelt Island.

The Queensboro Bridge

The Queensboro Bridge is an iconic suspension bridge that spans the

East River. Designed by architect Henry Hornbostel, it was inaugurated in 1909. During the marathon, runners cross the bridge westward, leaving Queens behind them. The ascent of the bridge is challenging, but the spectacular view of the Manhattan skyline makes the experience unforgettable. The Queensboro Bridge is a critical point of the race, as the climb and descent of the bridge can be extremely tiring. During the marathon, the lower level of the bridge is closed to traffic and is reserved for runners who find themselves in a sort of dark and silent gallery. Along the route, one can admire the Silvercup Studios, the largest film production facility in New York City. The facility has been used to shoot music videos, commercials, and movie scenes, including Highlander and Garbo Talks. Over the years, the use of the studio's space has shifted towards television series production, becoming the filming location for ABC's Hope & Faith, Sex and the City, and The Sopranos. The view from the top of the bridge is incredible, and many marathoners stop to take pictures. Manhattan

After the bridge, runners descend into the heart of New York: Manhattan. The marathon stretch along First Avenue is a unique experience with thousands of people welcoming the runners. That stretch of road is characterized by rolling hills that allow runners to admire the flow of marathoners. The First Avenue stretch is the point where runners enter the Upper East Side. The crowd gathering along the roads becomes even noisier. Runners find themselves facing a long road heading north. A stretch that extends from E 77th Street to E 96th Street. The view is spectacular, with tall buildings and majestic trees. This area is considered one of the most elegant in Manhattan. It's a challenging stretch, but the noisy and passionate crowd supporting the runners makes the experience unforgettable.

Harlem

Once past E 97th Street, runners cross an imaginary border between two different worlds, and the architecture reflects this difference. Luxury buildings disappear to give way to less opulent houses and public housing projects. But the cheering improves during the race. The positive energy, warmth, and enthusiasm are palpable. Even if there are fewer people on the streets, the level of celebration is even higher. Harlem shows all its Latin soul.

The race reaches the 30th kilometer and fatigue begins to be seriously felt, especially when tackling the uphill climb of the Willis Avenue Bridge, which brings the marathoners into the Bronx in the Mott Haven neighborhood.

The Willis Avenue Bridge was designed by architect Alfred Pancoast Boller and was built as a two-level structure, with an upper section for the subway and a lower one for vehicular traffic. It was the first suspension bridge built of steel and reinforced concrete. Over the years, it has undergone renovations, particularly after being severely damaged by Hurricane Sandy in 2012. Today, the Willis Avenue Bridge is one of the most spectacular parts of the New York Marathon route, as it offers participants and visitors a spectacular view of the East River and the skyscrapers.

Bronx

The Bronx is one of the five boroughs (districts) of New York City and is in the northern part of the city. Its history dates to the 17th century when the first Dutch settlers arrived in the region and founded the village of Bronck's Farm. The area was originally inhabited by indigenous tribes, including the Siwanoy and the Lenape. In 1874, it was incorporated as an independent town from Westchester city. With the expansion of the city, the Bronx became part of New York in 1898. Over the years, it has evolved through various economic and social cycles; between the '30s and '40s, it was one of the city's wealthiest areas. However, in the '60s and '70s, the economic situation rapidly deteriorated due to a series of factors, including unemployment, crime, and pollution. The crisis reached its peak in the '70s with the bankruptcy of New York City's government and in 1977 when a blackout caused a wave of violence and many lootings. This led to a massive flight of residents and businesses leaving the buildings in ruins.

In the '80s and '90s, the Bronx underwent a profound transformation thanks to urban redevelopment programs. The reconstruction made the district an important cultural, economic, and tourist center of New York City, famous for its zoo, Yankee Stadium, and the Bronx Museum of the Arts. Today, it's a vibrant place with a multi-ethnic population and a strong Latino and African American presence. The district is known for its strong cultural identity and its many celebrities, including Edgar Allan Poe, Jennifer Lopez, and Sonia Sotomayor.

As soon as the runners pass the bridge, they turn left onto E 135th

Street. They cross Mott Haven, named after the Mott family who owned a vast agricultural area here. Today, the neighborhood is a vibrant mix of multi-ethnic communities and new residents who appreciate its proximity to Manhattan and the Hudson River coast. In this area, spectators are sparse, with fewer people willing to cheer on the runners. But the volunteers handing out bananas, smiles, and pats on the back take care of it.

Before they have time to savor the buildings decorated with classic fire escape stairs, they are catapulted back into Manhattan, in Central Harlem on the famous Fifth Avenue where the incredible atmosphere overwhelms the runners, encouraging them to continue the race.

Museum Mile

In this area, the marathon route is characterized by a constant and challenging uphill climb. Along the road, runners pass the "Museum Mile," a section of Fifth Avenue that hosts some of the city's most important museums. It is named because it extends for about a mile and is located between 105th and 82nd Street. Museums include the Metropolitan Museum of Art, the Solomon R. Guggenheim Museum, the Museum of the City of New York, El Museo del Barrio, the Jewish Museum, Cooper Hewitt, Smithsonian Design Museum, Neue Galerie, and the African Center for Contemporary Art.

In this area, organized groups gather to fundraise for charities. They gather along the road to support their favorites and cheer them on before they disappear into Central Park.

Central Park

Central Park is one of the largest and most famous public parks in the world. Its history began in 1850 when the city administration decided to create a large public park in a sparsely populated area. The project was entrusted to talented but little-known landscape architects Olmsted and Vaux. It was built on an area of about 840 acres with the labor of thousands of Irish immigrants.

Olmsted and Vaux designed the park as a natural oasis in the heart of the city, with hills, lakes, waterfalls, meadows, gardens, and forests. They also constructed bridges, trails, an astronomical observatory, and even a medieval-style castle. Central Park soon became one of the favorite places for New Yorkers to take walks, have picnics, run, skate, and relax outdoors. Over the years, the park has also hosted concerts, political events, sports events, and various celebrations. Today, Central Park is an icon of the city, a meeting place and recreation area for tourists and residents. It is managed by the Central Park Conservancy, a nonprofit private organization that takes care of its maintenance and preservation. Once inside the park, marathoners head south along the East Drive, passing by the Jacqueline Kennedy Onassis Reservoir and the statue of Fred Lebow, the founder of the New York City Marathon.

Cleopatra's Needle

The autumn landscape and the presence of many spectators create a unique atmosphere. The route passes in front of "Cleopatra's Needle," a 21-meter-high Egyptian obelisk. It is one of the three remaining ancient examples in the world, along with those in London and Paris. It was originally erected in Egypt around 1450 BC during the reign of Pharaoh Thutmose III. In 1877, the American vice consul in London, William Henry Vanderbilt, donated it to the city as a sign of friendship between the United States and the United Kingdom.

After some ups and downs, the runners enter the park section known as Cat Hill, where the bronze statue called "Still Hunt" is located. It is a 2-meter-high artwork created by American sculptor Edward Kemeys and depicts a puma crouched on a rock, ready to pounce on its prey.
This is where the last three kilometers of the marathon begin. The stretch is hilly and particularly challenging. There is one final uphill that makes the exhausted marathoners feel the effort.

They reach the summit and suddenly find themselves on

Central Park South. A series of elegant buildings greet the runners. Less than a kilometer away, they arrive at Columbus Circle.

Columbus Circle

Columbus Circle is a Manhattan square located at the intersection of Central Park West, Eighth Avenue, Broadway, and Central Park South. Its construction dates to the late 19th century when New York City decided to restructure the chaotic road junction between Broadway and Eighth Avenue. The square was named "Columbus Circle" in honor of Christopher Columbus, in anticipation of the celebrations for the 400th anniversary of the discovery of the Americas. A monument was erected in the center to commemorate the Italian navigator.

Over the years, the square has undergone numerous

transformations and renovations, including a significant redesign in 2005 that resulted in the creation of a fountain and a pedestrian area. Today, it is one of the most famous areas of Manhattan and a major landmark of the city. It is surrounded by important buildings, including the Time Warner Center, CNN headquarters, and the New York City Opera. Additionally, the square is a major transportation hub with numerous bus lines and a subway station serving the A, B, C, D, and 1 line.

Back to Central Park

It's time to look up at the statue of Christopher Columbus, and it's already time to turn right and reenter Central Park. Here, runners pass an iconic sign that they will remember forever: "400 meters to go." Tears start to wet their faces, exhaustion fades away, and they begin to savor the finish line.

The last meters of the New York City Marathon are uphill, but it no longer matters if their legs ache or blisters have formed on their feet. It is in these moments that the individual stories of every marathoner are made.

The Final Steps

The final steps of the New York City Marathon are indescribable; each runner arrives with their own emotions. Some collapse to the ground, others raise their arms to the sky, some laugh or cry with happiness. There are those who remain rooted on their own legs. But one thing unites them all, from the first finisher to the last runner crossing the finish line: they are all winners. They are all heroes. They are all marathoners.

The New York City Marathon allows you to explore the world in a single race, crossing places that represent the most diverse languages, hundreds of traditions and religions, different smells, physical appearances, and somatic features. It is a challenging race, very difficult, but at the same time, exciting and rewarding.

The Finish

At the finish line, runners are welcomed by a large crowd of spectators who applaud and support them during the last meters of the race. The atmosphere is charged with energy as many runners raise their arms to the sky in triumph and victory.

Once they cross the finish line, the runners are greeted by volunteers from the organization who present them with participation medals and a thermal blanket to protect them from the cold. The atmosphere at the finish is special, capable of giving participants an unforgettable emotion and a sense of personal accomplishment that is difficult to describe in words.

Additionally, runners receive a bag with some food products and beverages. There are also places where the runners can relax, eat, and meet family and friends after the race.

The customary photo at Times Square with the medal hanging around the neck is a special moment. After running 42.195 kilometers through the five boroughs of New York, many runners choose to go there to take a photo. It is usually taken at night when the lights create a unique and colorful background. Participants position themselves in the middle of the street, raising the medal above their heads to show it to the world.

The Rules for Running the New York City Marathon

Rule 1

It's easy to fall into the temptation of exploring all the corners of New York, especially for runners visiting the city for the first time. But walking for hours and touring the city can be a serious mistake. This could lead to excessive exhaustion and fatigue caused by jet lag, which could negatively impact the runner's performance during the race. It's important to avoid wandering too much, especially on Saturday, and save energy for the race.

Rule 2

Choose the ferry instead of the bus to get to the marathon start because the scenic route in the New York Bay is exciting and the schedules are more "human-friendly." Additionally, when you arrive at Staten Island, you don't have to immediately exit the terminal. You can wait in the warmth until your scheduled start time.

Rule 3

The day of the New York City Marathon coincides with the end of daylight-saving time, offering an extra hour of sleep, but it can cause confusion with digital devices that automatically update the time. Relying on the alarm clock of a traditional watch is essential.

Rule 4

The TCS NYC Marathon bib contains a lot of useful information for participating in the race. It includes the start color, wave number, corral letter, and the runner's actual number. The color is important because the marathon has three distinct lines: blue, orange, and green, each with its own starting village. When runners arrive in Brooklyn, the three routes separate due to different exits from the bridge. Runners will follow different paths before reuniting later. The start wave is determined based on the declared times at registration, with starts every 25 minutes. Finally, the corral letter determines where the runner will enter the group relative to the wave. Bibs cannot be changed at the Expo, but runners can start in a later wave than their own, perhaps to join a friend. The blue bib starts on the right side of the bridge, on the upper level; the orange bib starts on the left side of the bridge, on the upper level; the green bib starts on the left side of the bridge, on the lower level.

Rule 5

From the moment you arrive at the marathon village until the start of the race, many hours can pass. You are often at the mercy of the cold, wind, and perhaps even rain. It's important to dress warmly using clothes that can be abandoned or better yet, donated. It is customary to place your clothes in designated bins, which will be donated to charity.

Rule 6

While waiting for the start of the New York City Marathon, there are some rules to follow: reach your assigned village, leave your baggage, and get to your assigned corral. You need to queue for each phase, so it's important to pay attention to the timing and schedule to avoid missing your wave. It takes at least 10-15 minutes to drop off the baggage and another 10 minutes to figure out where your corral is located. It's crucial not to be in a last-minute rush and end up without the opportunity to use the restroom. It may sound silly, but it's true. There are many bathrooms at the start, but the line is always long.

Rule 7

It's good to meet friends and family along the course. They provide motivation to keep running. You can use the smartphone application provided by the NYRR to plan meetups along the route near subway stations. Good points to meet your supporters are before the Queensboro Bridge in Queens, in the Bronx, in Central Park, and, of course, near the finish line.

Rule 8

During the marathon, it's advisable to avoid using headphones and listen to the music of the live bands and DJs along the course.

Moreover, the noise from the crowd will cover the sound playing from the earphones.

Rule 9

Upon reaching the finish line, there is an immediate push to keep moving. You pass through the medal area and the photo area. You receive a bag with food, supplements, fruit, various snacks, and a thermal blanket. You walk for about 20 minutes until you reach a junction. Here, you split. Those who chose the "No baggage" option will exit the park, while those who chose "Baggage" will continue walking towards the trucks to retrieve their bags. In any case, it will take 45-50 minutes to exit and meet your friends near Columbus Circle. It's better to notify them and arrange to meet in less crowded areas.

Rule 10

Avoid the venues near Columbus Circle; they will be crowded. Being able to grab a bite to eat may require waiting for hours. The advice is to move towards the Hudson River, along Broadway or Seventh and Eighth Avenue. As for transportation, taxis will be difficult to find, so it's better to take the subway or walk. The subway station is under Columbus Circle, and from there, you can reach any other junction.

Essential Rule

Wearing the medal around your neck is a way to stand out and be cheered by passersby even in the following days. It's best not to leave it in the hotel but to show it off in restaurants, parks, and major tourist attractions. Try it to believe it.

One Tip

To avoid leg pain, it's advisable to descend stairs in reverse, including those in the subway.

The New York City Marathon is more than just a race. It's a unique and extraordinary experience that goes beyond personal times and records. Taking on this challenging and complex course requires total commitment and an open attitude towards everything encountered along the way.

The beauty of this race lies in enjoying every single step, every neighborhood crossed, and marveling at the ever-changing city, kilometer after kilometer. Hearing your name shouted by a crowd of strangers is an priceless emotion.

It's important to pause and greet the children, thank the volunteers, and smile at the photographers capturing the most beautiful moments. Listening to the silence on the bridges, dancing to the music of the bands, and crying with happiness for making it. These are strong emotions that only those who have run the New York City Marathon can understand.

This race is much more than just a competition; it's an experience that should be fully embraced. There's nothing more rewarding than being able to say, "I ran the New York City Marathon" and becoming part of an exclusive club of runners who dream of participating every year.

Participants' Experiences

The New York City Marathon is one of the most famous races in the world, a test that requires courage, willpower, and limitless determination. But why do people subject themselves to such an exhausting and demanding challenge? What drives athletes to push beyond their physical and mental limits to complete the 42 kilometers and 195 meters of this legendary race?

Running a marathon represents an ambitious goal for many people, a test of strength and endurance that requires months of preparation. Crossing the finish line is like a personal victory, a demonstration of courage and determination that confirms the ability to overcome any obstacle.

The New York City Marathon is much more than just a race. It's an event that involves the entire city, a celebration of the culture and spirit of community that characterize the Big Apple. Every year, millions of people gather along the course to support the runners, creating a unique atmosphere that motivates athletes to keep going despite the fatigue.

Many people participate in the race to raise funds for charities. Runners offer their commitment and effort to support a good cause. This aspect of the race adds a dimension of altruism to the challenge, making the run an even more meaningful experience.

But beyond all these reasons, there is something even deeper that drives people to run the New York City Marathon. It's a challenge that goes beyond mere athletic performance and requires an energy that goes far beyond physicality. The American race tests the inner strength of individuals, their ability to overcome difficulties and withstand adversity.

Perhaps that's why so many people are drawn to the New York City Marathon. The race represents a challenge for the spirit as well. There is nothing more exciting than hearing the stories of those who have run the marathon with a particular goal in mind.

Each participant has a reason for running the marathon, whether it's for a charitable cause, to overcome a personal challenge, or simply to enjoy the unique atmosphere of the event.

The New York City Marathon changes lives, leaves a lasting impression on the memories of all who participate, and often becomes a landmark in the lives of many.

Mary's Story

Mary is a 35-year-old woman from Boston. She has run the New York City Marathon three times. For her, it has been an incredible experience. She has enjoyed the city's energy and the support of the fans along the course.

John's Story

John ran the New York City Marathon for the first time last year. The race coincided with his 45th birthday. His experience was filled with emotional highs and lows. The most challenging part was when he reached the Harlem Hills, which he described as "the most demanding part of the course." However, the view of Central Park and the support of the fans along the way helped him overcome the difficult moments.

Sarah's Story

Sarah, a 28-year-old, has run the New York City Marathon twice. The marathon helped her realize that it's possible to overcome any challenge with the right mindset and proper preparation.

Bob's Story

Bob is a 50-year-old man who has run the last ten editions of the marathon. It has become an annual tradition for him. He loves the city's energy and the support of the fans along the course.

Michael's Story

One of the participants, a young man named Michael, started running to lose weight. He weighed 145 kilograms. Over the two years of preparation, he lost 55 kilograms. He followed a targeted training program, gradually increasing distance and speed. He also worked on his nutrition, focusing on eating healthy and balanced foods. Michael completed the New York City Marathon in less than five hours.

Jessica's Story

Jessica prepared for the marathon while working full-time and raising her three children. She is a single mother; her husband left her after she became pregnant with their third child. She had to make sacrifices, waking up early in the morning to go for a run before preparing breakfast for her children and taking them to school. She also involved her diabetic mother, visiting her after training sessions and engaging in physical exercises and postural gymnastics together. The result is that Jessica ran the New York City Marathon while her mother improved her own physical condition and health.

David's Story

David had to overcome a knee injury to participate in the New York City Marathon. He underwent physical therapy sessions but never lost his determination and desire to complete the race. He approached the marathon with caution, managing to overcome the pain and successfully finish the race.

Maria's Story

The New York City Marathon changed Maria's life. She has always struggled with panic attacks. On the advice of her therapist, she started walking with a group of women from her neighborhood. Within a few months, brisk walks turned into slow and steady runs. She discovered that exercise helped her combat the anxiety she had lived with her whole life. She decided to participate in the New York City Marathon on the advice of her psychologist. She completed it and since then, Maria has been helping women going through difficult periods, uncertainty, and overwhelmed by anxiety. She has already accompanied ten of them to the finish line of the New York City Marathon, and now, at sixty years old, she is preparing for a new adventure in the American city.

Samantha's Story

After months of chemotherapy and radiation therapy, Samantha won her battle against cancer. She has always had a passion for running, but when she was diagnosed with cancer, she paused her training to focus on her health. Once she recovered, she felt it was time to start running again. She decided to register for the New York City

Marathon and began training with the help of her brother-in-law, a physical education teacher. Samantha found comfort in running. It became a form of meditation, a way to clear her mind. On the day of the marathon, she was nervous. During the race, she reflected on the period of illness and realized how strong she had been in her healing journey. She crossed the finish line exhausted but happy. Finishing the New York City Marathon proved to herself and the world that she can overcome any challenge. Samantha continued her training, became a mother, and now, at 46 years old, her passion for running has infected her entire family.

Terry's Story

The New York City Marathon attracts people from all over the world. Some of them, despite their physical difficulties, have never stopped dreaming of running the world's most important marathon. One example is Terry Fox, a young Canadian who lost a leg due to cancer. He decided to participate in the race to raise awareness and funds for cancer research. He was an extraordinary athlete. Despite his disability, he continued to train. He faced many challenges but never gave up. On the day of the New York City Marathon, Terry showed up at the start line with his prosthetic leg. The race was very tough. He fought through the pain and fatigue the entire time but never stopped running. His story became a symbol of hope and the fight against illness. Terry continued his battle by participating in other races. Unfortunately, his health deteriorated, and Terry left us, but his legacy lives on. He was the first runner with a prosthetic leg to run in New York. His story has inspired many others. Running a marathon is already an achievement in itself but doing it with a prosthetic leg is even more challenging. These athletes demonstrate that with the right attitude and determination, any obstacle can be overcome. They are an example for all of us, and we can find inspiration in their strength and resilience.

The Story of Jack

Many participants in the New York City Marathon run for a special cause or purpose. Jack, a 50-year-old man, decided to run the marathon to raise funds for Alzheimer's disease research. He witnessed the effects and symptoms on his father and decided to run the New York City Marathon to support all those who have had similar experiences. When he crossed the finish line, he felt overwhelmed with emotion. Jack continued to train and participate in other races in major cities in the United Kingdom. With the donations he collected, he opened a clinic to help patients and their families.

José's Story

José is a man with a mission that makes him a hero in the eyes of those who know him. His story is that of a father who wants to give hope to families fighting childhood cancer, a disease that was diagnosed in his daughter. She underwent long treatments and a delicate surgical procedure. Alejandra, that's her name, has recovered. José is a determined man who does not stop in the face of difficulties. He wanted to show gratitude to the people who helped him. He started collecting donations for childhood cancer research. Then he came up with the idea of running the marathon, using his story to serve charities. He trained hard in any weather conditions. Newspapers and media outlets covered his story, giving visibility to the fundraising campaign. The more the word spread, the more people donated. During the race, José continued to think about his mission and all the families fighting the disease. He fought with every breath to overcome obstacles. When he crossed the finish line, he cried tears of joy. José has given hope to those who struggle, showing that unity and solidarity can achieve a lot. He is a modern hero, a man who did not give up in the face of adversity, a courageous man seeking the common good.

John, Emily, Michele, Christensen's Stories

There are many people who choose to run the New York City Marathon to achieve an important goal, to support a cause. These runners see the marathon as a platform to raise awareness and funds. They are ready to run for kilometers and kilometers, pushing their limits to reach their goal.

John is a lawyer who ran the marathon to draw attention to the refugee crisis. He knows that words alone are not enough to solve the world's problems. He witnessed firsthand the suffering of people forced to flee their homes and decided to do his part. He ran to raise public awareness and collect funds for organizations that provide assistance to refugees. He paid tribute to those who are forced to flee from injustice and wars.

Emily is a young teacher. She knows that bullying can have a devastating impact on children's lives. She decided to run the marathon to raise funds for organizations working to prevent this social plague, raising awareness about the importance of creating a safe and welcoming environment for all children.

Michele, a civil rights activist, decided to run the marathon to draw attention to economic, racial, and social inequality. He created a crowdfunding campaign to raise funds for organizations operating in Africa.

Christensen, a biotechnology researcher, decided to run the marathon to raise funds for cancer research. He involved his colleagues and friends.

These runners who run for a cause in New York are the epitome of passion and determination. They carry on their social commitment, inspiring other runners to do the same.

Lisa's Story

The New York City Marathon is an opportunity to overcome difficulties. Lisa is a brave and determined woman. She decided to participate in the marathon after losing her father, who died by suicide two years earlier. The loss of a parent is already a traumatic event, but the fact that Lisa's father took his own life made the situation even more difficult. She had already lost her mother in a tragic car accident. At only twenty years old, she found herself dealing with an immeasurable pain, economic problems, and eviction. She felt alone, powerless, without the strength to move forward. But then something changed. She started hanging out with a group of girls from her neighborhood who had a passion for running. After a few weeks, she decided to run the New York City Marathon, not only to honor her parents' memory but also to find the strength to overcome her suffering and give meaning to her life. She started training hard, running for kilometers and kilometers, trying to release the anger and sadness that consumed her. She tried to focus on running, on the effort, on the sweat flowing on her skin, trying to forget the pain and find some inner peace. The marathon was a difficult test for Lisa, a titanic feat that required every ounce of energy and determination. She felt the pain in her legs, the fatigue in her breathing, the urge to give up. When she crossed the finish line, Lisa felt a sense of liberation and happiness that momentarily made her forget her pain. She realized she had done something great, surpassed her limits, and proved to herself that she was stronger than she thought. The New York City Marathon didn't erase her pain or solve all her problems, but it gave her the strength and courage to move forward, to look to the future with hope and trust. It showed her that running can also be a therapy for the soul, a way to find oneself. Lisa's story circulated throughout the city. Her determination convinced an entrepreneur to hire her at a shipping agency and pay for her studies. She graduated and now teaches history at a public school in Los Angeles. Thanks to her popularity, she founded a charity to help children of deceased parents finish their studies.

Sara's Story

The New York City Marathon is an event that attracts thousands of runners from around the world, each with their own motivation, their own reason to run. There is a woman who has a particularly touching story, one that evokes deep emotions and demonstrates the strength of the human spirit in the face of life's tragedies. Sara is a courageous and determined woman. She decided to participate in the New York City Marathon after battling alcoholism for most of her life. It was a monster that devoured her from within, leading her to despair and loneliness. She lost her job, the love of her life, and many friends. But one day, she decided that it was time to change her life and find the strength to fight back. She sought help and enrolled in a rehabilitation program where she met other people going through the same struggle. During her journey, she discovered running as a form of therapy and liberation. She started training on the country roads in northern Spain. Through running, she found an escape from her inner demons and a strength she didn't think she possessed. The New York City Marathon was an opportunity for Sara to prove to herself that she could overcome difficulties. Unfortunately, a sharp pain in her calf forced her to withdraw. But she didn't give up. She trained consistently and completed the race the following year. In those two years of commitment and sacrifice, Sara overcame her alcoholism. Her determination didn't stop there; her commitment continues. She became a volunteer in the group that supported her. Now, she helps people overcome addiction through physical activity and sports. Running has given her a new life and the opportunity to rebuild everything that alcoholism had taken away.

Markus's Story

There is something extraordinarily powerful in the ability to overcome difficulties, to lift oneself above one's adversities and find the strength to pursue one's dreams. That's what Markus did, a man who experienced the dark side of being human, with an inner battle that brought him to the edge of the abyss. His life took a dramatic turn at a young age when he started using drugs. Experimentation turned into an obsession that swallowed him, leaving him without a job, without friends, and without hope. His life became a cycle of misery and failures, with drug addiction continuing to dominate his existence. The turning point came during a rehabilitation experience, where he had the chance to meet other people fighting the same difficulties. He started running, finding the strength to resist temptations and the urge to use drugs. That newfound passion allowed him to rediscover a part of himself that seemed lost. But running wasn't just a way to escape problems; it was a way to confront them. While running, Markus started his therapy, conquering fears and uncertainties. After staying in a community on the outskirts of Berlin, he decided to change his life. He went to live in France with his sister Agatha. He found a job at a supermarket and continued running until he participated in the Paris Half Marathon. During that race, Markus fell and fractured his right wrist. Agatha understood his difficulties and registered him for the New York City Marathon, which he ran the following year. However, Markus wanted to do more. His participation in the marathon was also a way to help those who struggle and fight against addiction. For these people, Markus became an example of hope. He brings his experience to recovery communities, spreading a message of hope, strength, and determination.

John's Story

The New York City Marathon is much more than just a race. For many people, it represents an opportunity to honor the memory of a loved one. It's a way to express grief but also to celebrate life and love. John decided to run the marathon in memory of his life partner. One day, the illness struck her and took her away in a brutal and unexpected manner. John decided to transform his pain into something positive by enrolling in the race in the American city. He created a personalized shirt with his partner's photo and name, as if she were running by his side. It was a way to honor her memory and celebrate the love they had shared. This is just one of the many stories of runners who have run the marathon in memory of a loved one. Some participated in the marathon to remember a parent, a child, a friend, or a relative who fought against a disease. The marathon can be a way to find comfort and hope in a difficult moment of life. Running the New York City Marathon is not just a physical matter but a matter of inner strength. It requires great determination, passion, and motivation. And when running in memory of a loved one, the motivation comes straight from the heart.

The story of David

The New York Marathon is one of the most prestigious and challenging races in the world, and it is certainly not an easy feat. But for those who have decided to take on the challenge in a wheelchair, the stakes are even higher, filled with obstacles.

David is a young athlete who has decided to run in New York. His story is filled with determination and perseverance: he lost the use of his legs after a serious car accident. For David, running the New York Marathon was a dream. He had already participated in other wheelchair races, but he knew that the marathon would be the biggest challenge of his life. He started training hard, putting his willpower to the test. The day of the race was full of mixed emotions. On one hand, there was his excitement; on the other hand, there was the awareness that it would be an extremely exhausting and demanding race, with the risk of encountering difficulties along the way.

But David did not get discouraged. He breezed through the first few kilometers, utilizing the strength of his arms. Then came the fatigue, the uphill climbs, the rough patches. It wasn't just a test of physical endurance; it was also a test of mental strength and resilience. He had to face moments of discouragement and pain. But there was also the thrill of reaching the finish line after seven hours of exertion. David crossed the finish line with his arms raised to the sky and tears in his eyes.

The New York Marathon is a challenging race not only for able-bodied individuals. Many wheelchair athletes participate, showcasing great determination. To reach the finish line, they require proper physical and mental preparation.

The stories of Simon, Michael, Brad, Charlie

If running a marathon can be a challenge for anyone, for a person with visual impairments, it becomes even more difficult.

Simon Wheatcroft is a blind ultramarathon runner. He lost his sight at the age of 17 due to a degenerative eye disease. Despite his blindness, he continued to run, using a sound navigation system. Wheatcroft participated in the New York Marathon as part of the "With A Vision" team, a group of blind athletes. They run to raise funds for organizations that strive to improve the lives of people with visual disabilities.

Michael Stone, another blind ultramarathon runner, also ran the New York Marathon. He gradually lost his vision due to a genetic disease, but he kept running and participating in road races and triathlons, using another runner as his guide.

Brad Snyder is former military personnel who lost his sight following an explosion in Afghanistan, while Charlie Plaskon is blind due to a degenerative eye disease. Both completed the New York Marathon.

For visually impaired runners, running can be an even greater challenge, but thanks to technology and guide runners, these athletes complete the race alongside thousands of other runners. Their perseverance and determination are an example for everyone.

THE MEANING OF THE NEW YORK MARATHON

The New York Marathon is much more than just a race. It is an event that draws people from all over the world, united by a passion for challenge and achievement. It is a life-changing experience that gives strength to surpass one's limits.

People come to New York for different reasons, but they all share one thing in common: the desire to make it. Whether you are an experienced runner or an amateur runner taking on this distance for the first time, the feeling of crossing the finish line after 42.195 kilometers will be a unique emotion. In that moment, the pain and fatigue will be replaced by a wave of euphoria and satisfaction. It will be an unforgettable experience.

The New York Marathon is a celebration of diversity and inclusion, an opportunity to explore the wonders of the American city and meet people from all over the world. It is a demonstration of resilience, humanity, and solidarity. Its preparation requires commitment, dedication, and a lot of sweat. But the satisfaction felt when crossing the finish line is incomparable.

It is a one-of-a-kind event, a celebration of life itself, the ability to overcome challenges and achieve seemingly impossible goals. It is an opportunity to prove to ourselves and the world that there is nothing we cannot do if we truly commit to it. It is an experience that will remain etched in the mind forever.

It must be run with heart, with all one's soul. The finish line must be crossed with a smile on one's lips. The victory is yours. No one can ever take away this incredible feeling.

Never Give Up

Printed in Great Britain
by Amazon

57662288R00076